LOVED

Fruit Of The Spirit Series

LOVED

Transformed by God's Love, Empowered to Love Others.

DR. CHIZOBAM IDAHOSA

Library of Congress Cataloging-in-Production data on file at the
Library of Congress, Washington, DC
ISBN: 979-8-9933388-0-4
Cover Design: Oktionz Images
Text layout and Design: GFEC Press

DEDICATION

To God, who loves me unconditionally, set me apart, named me, and called me even before I was born, while I was still in my mother's womb.

Contents

Introduction

The fruit of the Spirit is the outward expression of God's nature within. It is the way of life for those who are led by the Spirit of God. These fruit—love, joy, peace, patience, kindness, goodness, faithfulness, gentleness, and self-control—are not merely moral ideals; they are signs of growth and maturity in a Christian and the product of a Spirit-controlled life (Galatians 5:22–23).

This book is the first in the "Fruit of the Spirit Series" a collection dedicated to exploring each of the nine fruit and the vital role the Holy Spirit plays as our Helper as He transforms us into the image of Christ.

We begin with love, because love is foundational. Every other fruit flows out of it.

God's love is both unconditional and immeasurable. It comforts, refreshes, corrects, and strengthens us. His love accepts us as we are, transforms us, and brings healing to our brokenness and trauma. God's love is always available.

However, to fully embrace it—and truly share it with others—we must remain in Him.

This means spending time in His presence, praying, staying rooted in His Word, and choosing to walk in obedience daily. It is through this abiding relationship that His love takes deeper root in our hearts and begins to flow naturally to those around us.

Walking in love didn't come naturally to me. But through the help and guidance of the Holy Spirit, I have learned, I am learning, and continue to learn how to love God and love others. This book reflects my journey—what I've discovered about receiving God' love and allowing it to flow through me to those around me.

I invite you to join me through these pages, as we learn together how to receive God's love more deeply, and reflect that love to the world with the help of the Holy Spirit.

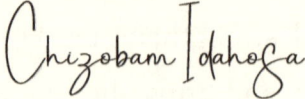

1

God's Love Empowers Us To Love Others

"And we have known and believed the love that God has for us. God is love, and he who abides in love abides in God, and God in him."

~ I John 4:16 NKJV

Walking in love did not come naturally to me at all. Don't get me wrong, I was good at loving those who loved me back. I simply did not "waste" time and emotions on the difficult people in my life.

After I was born-again, God began to plow my heart, and I matriculated into the "University of the God-kind of love." In His infinite wisdom and patience, God repeatedly positioned me to be in proximity to people who tripped me up. In hindsight, I now realize He was training me to exercise my love muscles so that I could grow and mature in love.

I failed so many of those love tests that I lost count. Although I intended to obey God's command to love others, I kept yielding to my selfishness and losing my patience with impunity. At one point, I stopped trying. Once God brought someone unloving my way, I subconsciously graded myself as a failure immediately. I decided there was no point engaging since I was going to fail anyway.

Finally, through the guidance of the Holy Spirit, it dawned on me that I could not express love in difficult situations because I had not received God's love for myself. My identity was based on all sorts of things, but not on who I was in Christ. I didn't see myself as "the disciple who Jesus loved" (John 13:23).

I lacked the revelation of abiding in the love of God. Therefore, my life was not built and sustained on the foundation of God's love for me.

How could I give what I didn't have?

God's Love in Us

I did have God's love within me. The Word makes it clear in Romans 5:5 that all believers have the love of God in their hearts. The problem was that I wasn't tapping into His love. Instead, I was blocking it from flowing through me to others.

You can't love people out of a vacuum. God is love! Love is who He is. Therefore, your love for people flows from the overflow of God's love for you. You must know Him intimately and understand His love for you before you can give love to others. 1 John 4:8 puts it this way: "Whoever does not love does not know God, because God is love." God has shown you His love so that you can love others the same way He loves you.

Three Crucial Questions

So, I have 3 questions for you. Do you:

1. Believe God loves you personally and intimately?

2. Love Him back?

3. Love others with the same love you have received from God?

The rest of this chapter focuses on God's love for us.

In the next chapters, we will discuss what the Word teaches on obeying God's command to walk in the fruit of love.

I pray that as we consistently meditate on these Scriptures, our revelation of God's love for us will deepen and flourish, resulting in an outpouring of His love for others and a demonstration of His power and presence in our daily lives. In Jesus' name, Amen.

TEN SCRIPTURAL WAYS GOD'S LOVE EMPOWERS US TO LOVE OTHER

1. GOD IS LOVE

> "And we have known and believed the love that God has for us. God is love, and he who abides in love abides in God, and God in him." 1 John 4:16 NKJV

> "Anyone who does not love does not know God, because God is love."1 John 4:8 ESV

God is synonymous with love. When we spend time in His presence, we abide in love, grow to know Him more intimately, and allow His love to thaw our cold hearts. The more we abide in Him, the deeper our understanding of His love for us becomes.

Therefore, when you read His Word, read it as a love letter from Him.

He speaks in love, encourages through love, corrects, disciplines, and empowers in love. Everything He does, including His judgment of sin and disobedience, is built on the foundation of His love for the whole world.

Prayer: Lord, knowing that You are love, gives me peace and confidence to trust in Your promises and approach You without fear. In Jesus' name, Amen.

2. GOD LOVED US FIRST.

> "In this the love of God was made manifest among us, that God sent his only Son into the world, so that we might live through him. In this is love, not that we have loved God but that he loved us and sent his Son to be the propitiation for our sins. Beloved, if God so loved us, we also ought to love one another." 1 John 4:9–11 ESV

"But God shows his love for us in that while we were still sinners, Christ died for us." Romans 5:8 ESV

"We love because he first loved us." 1 John 4:19 ESV

The primary way God demonstrated His love for us was by sending Jesus to die on the cross for our sins. Jesus was crucified for unlovable, undeserving sinners. We were all doomed to eternal damnation, but God took the form of a man and came to earth to reconcile us to Himself, establishing a peaceful relationship through Christ (Philippians 2:6–8). He didn't need us, but He chose to relate to us intimately.

Prayer: Thank you, Lord, for loving me first while I was still Your enemy. Help me draw from Your love daily to love myself and others, even the difficult people You place in my path. In Jesus' name, Amen.

3. God Expressed His Love By Giving Us The Best Gift

"For God so loved the world, that he gave his only Son, that whoever believes in him should not perish but have eternal life." John 3:16 ESV

"This is how we know what love is: Jesus Christ laid down his life for us. And we ought to lay down our lives for our brothers and sisters." 1 John 3:16 NIV

"This is how God showed his love among us: He sent his one and only Son into the world that we might live through him." 1 John 4:9 NIV

God loves us so much that He gave His Son to save us from sin and death. Jesus Christ laid down His life to show us what unrestrained love looks like. He died on the cross and shed His blood to wash away our sins (Revelation 1:5). Since God already willingly gave us the ultimate gift of all, there's no reason for Him to withhold anything from us (Romans 8:32).

As we yield to God's love, the power of Christ—who lives in us—enables and empowers us to show love to others.

Prayer: Thank you, Jesus, for loving me so much that you gave your life to save me from the penalty of my sins. Amen.

"God loved you first. Allow this truth to marinate in your spirit consistently. Your love for God and others flows from God's love for you."

---

4. God's Love Changed Our Identity

"See what great love the Father has lavished on us, that we should be called children of God! And that is what we are!" 1 John 3:1a NIV

"He brought me to the banqueting house, and his banner over me was love." Song of Songs 2:4 NKJV

In ancient times, a banner was a:

† visible symbol of identity and allegiance,

† rallying point in battle or celebration, and

† sign of covering or protection.

Just as a banner in the physical world signals who you are and what you stand for, God's banner of love signifies belonging and protection. His banner over you is love. Therefore, you are known by God and recognized by the evidence of His love in your life.

Because of His great love for you, God changed your identity. You were once an oppressed sinner, but now, you are the child of the Most-High God.

He placed a banner over you as a signal to every spiritual power that you now belong to His family (and you know that no one jokes around with God's child).

I encourage you to do whatever it takes to consistently remind yourself that the creator of the universe is your Father. You can repeat these Scriptures multiple times. Shout, sing, or write them down until they resonate in your spirit.

Declaration: I am a child of the Most-High God.

5. God Loves Us the Same Way He Loves Jesus

> "I in them and You in Me, in order that they may become one and perfectly united, that the world may know and [definitely] recognize that You sent me and that You have loved them [even] as You have loved me."
> John 17:23 AMPC

The Scripture above, spoken by Jesus, presents a mind-blowing truth that we must never ignore: the creator of the universe loves us just as He loves His Son.

Prayer: Thank you, Lord, for loving me with the depth, height, and breadth of love that You love Jesus. Help me to understand how to walk in the fullness of this revelation. In Jesus' name, Amen.

6. GOD'S LOVE IS UNQUENCHABLE

"Who shall separate us from the love of Christ? Shall trouble or hardship or persecution or famine or nakedness or danger or sword? As it is written: "For your sake we face death all day long; we are considered as sheep to be slaughtered." No, in all these things we are more than conquerors through him who loved us.

For I am convinced that neither death nor life, neither angels nor demons, neither the present nor the future, nor any powers, neither height nor depth, nor anything else in all creation, will be able to separate us from the love of God that is in Christ Jesus our Lord." Romans 8:35-39 NIV

"For the mountains may move and the hills disappear, but even then my faithful love for you will remain. My covenant of blessing will never be broken, says the Lord, who has mercy on you." Isaiah 54:10 NLT

The love of God enables us to overcome all barriers: trouble, hardship, suffering, danger, and even death. No demon in hell or power on earth can withstand His love for us. As impossible as it may seem for mountains to move, God's faithful love for us will remain intact even if they do move.

Prayer: Help me, Lord, to have faith in Your love even when I'm going through an impossible situation. Help me never to forget that You are always for me, defending me and fighting for me. Your love for me never ends. In Jesus' name, Amen.

7. God's Love is Unconditional

"But when the kindness and love of God our Savior appeared, he saved us, not because of righteous things we had done, but because of his mercy. He saved us through the washing of rebirth and renewal by the Holy Spirit."
Titus 3:4-5 NIV

"But God, being rich in mercy, because of the great love with which he loved us, even when we were dead in our trespasses, made us alive together with Christ—by grace you have been saved." Ephesians 2:4-5 ESV

Prayer: Thank you, Lord, for loving me unconditionally, not because I deserved it, but because of who You are. In Jesus' name, Amen.

8. GOD'S LOVE IS EVERLASTING

> "Oh give thanks to the Lord, for he is good, for his steadfast love endures forever!" Psalm 107:1 ESV

> "The Lord appeared to us in the past, saying: I have loved you with an everlasting love; I have drawn you with unfailing kindness." Jeremiah 31:3 NIV

God's love for us lasts forever. It is consistent, uninterrupted, with no expiration date. He does not take a break from loving us. Every morning when we wake up, we are assured of His love.

Prayer: Lord, I am so grateful that Your love for me is dependable and unfailing. Thank you for remaining the same, even when I change. You are a good, good Father. In Jesus' name, Amen.

"God's love for us is an expression of His mercy and grace toward us. We don't deserve it, we can never earn it, but He pours it out anyway."

---

9. God is Excited About Loving Us

> "The Lord, your God, is with you, the Mighty Warrior who saves. He will take great delight in you; in his love, he will no longer rebuke you, but will rejoice over you with singing."
> Zephaniah 3:17 NIV

God is not mad at His children. He doesn't keep His love for us a secret. Instead, He showers His love on us, delights over us, and infuses our hearts with joy, gladness, and thanksgiving.

Declaration: God is not out to get me. He is delighted to be in a loving relationship with me.

10. God's Love Overcomes Fear and Condemnation

The revelation of God's love has empowered me to say NO to the condemnation of the enemy. If Christ died for me while I was steeped in sin, how much more does He love me now? I am God's elect. Jesus Christ himself speaks for me in the presence of God (Romans 8:32–34).

I am no longer petrified if I fail because I know that God's perfect love drives out fear (1 John 4:18). He has granted me permission to enter His throne room with my yuckiness and exchange it for His mercy and grace (Hebrews 4:16). Through the Holy Spirit, He counsels, trains, and guides me. His love for me washed my sins away so that His love through me can overlook and forgive the sins of others (1 Peter 4:8).

ACCEPTING GOD'S LOVE BY FAITH

I encourage you (and me) to fully believe and trust in God's love. Accept it by faith. Act as if it is irrevocably true. Meditate on these Scriptures, allowing them to become ingrained in your subconscious until you no longer question them.

Renew your mind so that your knee-jerk reactions to life's challenges (and people) will consistently be in the direction of God's love.

I have learned and continue to learn that my ability to love is an expression of my relationship with God. As I abide in Him and His Word abides in me, the Holy Spirit empowers me to love others. God gave me the Holy Spirit as my Helper, Comforter, Advocate, and Intercessor. The Holy Spirit is not out to get me by failing me on my love tests. When I mess up (and I still do), we talk. He tells me how and when I missed the mark and encourages me to press on for the prize (Philippians 3:14). I have yielded myself to Him; therefore, I am growing in love from one level of glory to another.

And this journey isn't just mine—it's yours too, if you want it. The same Holy Spirit who helps me grow in love is ready to walk with you, teach you, and strengthen you. As you lean into Him and let His word shape your heart, you'll begin to see real change–from the inside out. Love will no longer feel like a burden, but a response to the One who loved you first. It's a daily walk, but with God, it's possible.

PRAYER

I pray for you in the words of Apostle Paul, "that you, being rooted and established in love, may have power, together with all the Lord's holy people, to grasp how wide and long and high and deep is the love of Christ, and to know this love that surpasses knowledge–that you may be filled to the measure of all the fullness of God" (Ephesians 3:17–19 NIV). Amen.

REFLECT

✝ Have you come to understand that everything God does is rooted in His love for you?

✝ Do you truly believe that God loves you personally and intimately? How will this understanding of His love change the way you live today?

✝ What aspects of God's love have surprised or challenged you the most?

† Knowing that the Lord's love never fails, how can that encourage and strengthen you in what you're facing today?

† In what ways do you reflect God's love in how you treat others?

2

God Loves Us As He Loves Jesus Christ

The Bible is filled with profound truths about who God is and who we are to Him. However, there are specific Scriptures that I find particularly breathtaking.

In John 17, as Jesus prayed for all believers before His crucifixion, He prayed that we, the body of Christ, would experience complete unity so that the world would know that God loves us just as He loves Him, Jesus.

> "I have given to them the glory and honor which You have given me, that they may be one [even] as We are one: I in them and You in Me, in order that they may become one and perfectly united, that the world may know and [definitely] recognize that You sent me and that You have loved them [even] as You have loved me."
>
> John 17:22–23 AMPC

"God proved His infinite love for us by sending Jesus, whom He dearly loved, to the cross to die in our place."

The Scripture above is an astounding truth for us to believe and live by—to know with certainty that the Creator of the Universe loves us as He loves His Son.

As I reflected on how amazing it is to be loved by God, just as He loves Jesus, I decided to go to the Word to discover how God demonstrated this enormous, immeasurable love to us.

Here's what I found.

God Gave Jesus to Us as a Gift

"But God shows his love for us in that while we were still sinners, Christ died for us." Romans 5:8 ESV

Typically, we show our love to others by spending time with them, attending to their needs, and showering them with gifts and favors.

And we did not even deserve it! God gave us the gift of Jesus' life while we were still in our sinful state. The same Jesus He loved so deeply, He sacrificed for us on the cross. If that is not proof that God loves us as He loves Jesus, then I do not know what else can be more convincing.

"Jesus loves us as the Father loves Him"

Jesus, who is not only the Son of God but also the visible image of the invisible God (Colossians 1:15) and His perfect representation (Hebrews 1:3), also expressed that He loves us as the Father loves Him.

> "As the Father has loved me, so have I loved you. Abide in my love." John 15:9 ESV

God continues to demonstrate His love toward us through the Holy Spirit. God poured His love into our hearts to overflow when we put our faith in Jesus Christ (Romans 5:5). It is the power of God's love in our hearts that keeps us from losing hope in life. Instead, we are empowered to obey God's command to love Him with all our being and to love others as ourselves.

PRAYER

Thank you, Father, for loving me with the depth, height, and breadth of love that You have for Jesus. Reveal to me Your infinite love for me. Teach me to think and act as if You love me, and help me love others through the power of Your Spirit. In Jesus' name, Amen!

REFLECT

† Do you believe that God loves you as He loves Jesus?

† Have you opened your heart wide to receive the fullness of God's astounding love?

† Do you love God back?

† Are you remaining and dwelling in God's love and allowing it to overflow to others?

3

Love Is A Command. Not A Suggestion.

Since becoming a follower of Jesus Christ, the most crucial lesson I have learned, am learning, and will continue to learn is how to love God and love others.

Our primary focus is to understand the depth of God's love for us, as it is His love that empowers us to reciprocate and extend that love to others. When we genuinely receive God's love, it transforms us and overflows to those around us. Consequently, bearing the fruit of love becomes naturally supernatural for us because it is fueled by God's love.

"We love because he first loved us." 1 John 4:19 NIV

Next, we need to acknowledge that love is our primary command from God. A command is an order given by a superior authority that requires obedience. Walking in love is of first importance to God and, therefore, should be to us as well.

"Walking in love is of first importance to God and, therefore, should be to us as well."

It is not an option, suggestion, or request. To put it bluntly, if we are not walking in love, we are disobeying God.

When a Pharisee approached Jesus and asked Him what the greatest command of the law is, Jesus responded by saying:

> "Love the Lord your God with all your heart and with all your soul and with all your mind.' This is the first and greatest commandment. And the second is like it: 'Love your neighbor as yourself.' All the Law and the Prophets hang on these two commandments." Matthew 22:37–40 NIV

To love God is to obey Him (John 14:23; 1 John 5:3; 2 John 1:6), and obeying Him keeps us united with Him and protected by His love (John 15:9–10). When we love God, we are all in with no holding back. We become fully yielded to Him and His purpose for our lives. It becomes less about checking off boxes and more about following Him wholeheartedly—not out of compulsion.

WHY DID JESUS COMMAND US TO LOVE?

Jesus made love a command because others will recognize that we are God's children and become drawn into His kingdom by observing our loving actions. If we fail to love, we do not align with our responsibility as ambassadors for Christ.

> "A new command I give you: Love one another. As I have loved you, so you must love one another. By this everyone will know that you are my disciples, if you love one another."
> John 13:34-35 NIV

How effective would we be as Christ's ambassadors if we tell everyone at work that we are Christians but then exude a critical and judgmental spirit full of envy and strife?

Apostle John, who referred to himself multiple times as "the disciple whom Jesus loved," must have known without a doubt how much he was loved by Jesus. (See John 13:23; John 19:26; John 20:2.) Having personally experienced God's love, he reminded us several times in his letters to obey God's command to love.

Reflect and meditate on the Scriptures listed below, all written by the Apostle John in his letters to the early churches.

> "Whoever says, "I know him," but does not do what he commands is a liar, and the truth is not in that person. But if anyone obeys his word, love for God is truly made complete in them. This is how we know we are Whoever claims to live in him must live as Jesus did." 1 John 2:4-6 NIV

"And this is his command: to believe in the name of his Son, Jesus Christ, and to love one another as he commanded us. The one who keeps God's commands lives in him, and he in them. And this is how we know that he lives in us: We know it by the Spirit he gave us." 1 John 3:23-24 NIV

"And he has given us this command: Anyone who loves God must also love their brother and sister." 1 John 4:21 NIV

"This is how we know that we love the children of God: by loving God and carrying out his commands. In fact, this is love for God: to keep his commands. And his commands are not burdensome." 1 John 5:2-3 NIV

"And now, dear lady, I am not writing you a new command but one we have had from the beginning. I ask that we love one another. And this is love: that we walk in obedience to his commands. As you have heard from the beginning, his command is that you walk in love." 2 John 1:5-6 NIV

WALKING IN LOVE FULFILLS THE COMMANDS OF THE LAW

Going back to Jesus' response to the Pharisee, notice that Jesus said that "All the Law and the Prophets hang on these two commandments" (Matthew 22:40). By saying this, Jesus made it clear to His listeners that as they walk in love, they would, by default, keep all the commands of the law. They would no longer have to keep track of their obedience to each regulation of the Ten Commandments since walking in love fulfills them all.

Apostle Paul also underscored this truth in Romans 13

> "Let no debt remain outstanding, except the continuing debt to love one another, for whoever loves others has fulfilled the law. The commandments, "You shall not commit adultery," "You shall not murder," "You shall not steal," "You shall not covet," and whatever other command there may be, are summed up in this one command: "Love your neighbor as yourself." Love does no harm to a neighbor. Therefore, love is the fulfillment of the law." Romans 13:8-10 NIV

In our current dispensation, we are no longer obligated to adhere to the laws of the Old Covenant.

"To love God is to obey Him, and obeying Him keeps us united with Him and protected by His love."

We do not need to strive diligently to follow rules and regulations to be saved, attain righteousness, and maintain a relationship with God. Jesus Christ ushered in the New Covenant through His death, burial, and resurrection. We are saved by grace through our faith in Jesus Christ, not by keeping the law (Galatians 2:16, 21; 3:11 Ephesians 2:8–9).

However, we are still required to obey Jesus' command to love God and love others because God is love (1 John 4:8,16). Our faith in God and His Word works when it is powered and energized by love. True faith is active and expresses itself through love because love is the evidence and outflow of genuine faith (Galatians 5:6). Furthermore, love is eternal and can never be done away with (1 Corinthians 13:8,13).

LOVE YOUR NEIGHBOR AS YOURSELF

"Love the Lord your God with all your heart and with all your soul and with all your mind and with all your strength.' The second is this: 'Love your neighbor as yourself.' There is no commandment greater than these." Mark 12:30–31 NIV

Jesus commands that we love others as we love ourselves. This means that to love others effectively, we must first cultivate a healthy love for ourselves. We care for our needs, protect ourselves, and avoid harming ourselves. We should also extend the same care and consideration to others.

I also believe that loving ourselves involves understanding who we are in Christ. It is nearly impossible to love others well if we are burdened by self-pity and low self-esteem.

When our identity is rooted in Christ, we shed unhealthy thought patterns. We stop relying on others for constant validation and cease judging and criticizing ourselves. We can look in the mirror with confidence and say, "I am fearfully and wonderfully made," even if we see wrinkles, because we know our Father is pleased with us (Psalm 139:14 ESV).

Loving ourselves also involves establishing healthy boundaries, which helps us stay energized and fulfill the tasks that God has called us to. Jesus did not engage in every single problem during His earthly ministry. On one specific occasion, someone asked Jesus to intervene in a family inheritance dispute. His response was, "Who made me a judge or arbitrator over you?" (Luke 12:14 ESV). Jesus did not come to be a human judge; it was not His role to settle family disputes.

He came to give us eternal life, and He remained true to His mission of love (John 10:10).

The main objective of this chapter is to remind us that God has commanded us to walk in love. Next, we will explore the attributes of love by addressing the question, "What does biblical love look like?"

PRAYER

Lord, thank you for loving me and for giving me commands and instructions that protect and guide my path in life. I commit to obeying Your Word and trusting Your ways. Help me yield to the power of the Holy Spirit, so that Your love within me flows freely to those around me. Teach me to reflect Your heart in all I do. In Jesus' name, Amen.

REFLECT

† Have you always acknowledged love as a primary command from God?

† How does viewing love as a command, rather than a feeling or option, change the way you approach your relationships?

† Is the love you give a true reflection of your standing as Christ's ambassador?

† In what areas of your life do you find it most challenging to love others as God commands, and why?

† What steps can you take today to intentionally obey God's command to love, even when it's difficult or inconvenient?

4

What Does Biblical Love Look Like?

Jesus is Our Perfect Example of Love

Jesus commands us to love others as He loves us. And He loves us sacrificially and unconditionally. He willingly shed His blood and gave His life on the cross for us (John 15:12–13). While Jesus was physically on earth, He exemplified God's love. Jesus demonstrated His love for God by obeying Him. (See John 6:38; 12:49-50; 14:30-31; 15:10.)

Jesus showed compassion to people. He did not isolate Himself from crowds or turn a blind eye to people's needs by selfishly enforcing His personal space or "me time." Jesus understood the difference between true rest (which we all need) and self-centeredness. He replenished Himself through prayer (Matthew 14:22-23) and rest. However, He also knew when to sacrifice His rest in favor of serving others (Mark 6:30-34).

"Jesus commands us to love others as He loves us. And He loves us sacrificially and unconditionally.

It was out of love and compassion that Jesus:

✝ healed the sick – Matthew 14:14

✝ fed 4,000 hungry men (besides women and children) –
   Matthew 15:32; Mark 8:2

✝ healed the blind – Matthew 20:34

✝ taught the crowd and later fed the 5,000 – Mark 6:34–44

Therefore, just like Jesus, our love for one another should be self-giving rather than self-centered. We ought to be more concerned about the well-being of others than about our own comfort—laying down our lives for others, as Jesus did for us (1 John 3:16–18).

> "Therefore be imitators of God, as beloved children.
> And walk in love, as Christ loved us and gave himself up for
> us, a fragrant offering and sacrifice to God."
> Ephesians 5:1–2 ESV

TEN CHARACTERISTICS OF BIBLICAL LOVE

Here are ten characteristics of love pulled from the New Testament. As you review the list, ask the Holy Spirit to reveal areas where you need to grow and develop.

The good news is that although none of us will attain a perfect score, we can all grow and mature in love (Philippians 1:9; 2 Thessalonians 1:3).

Love...	
Honors Others	Romans 12:9-10
Is sincere and pure	Romans 12:9; 1 Peter 1:22
Never harms anyone	Romans 13:10
Is humble, gentle and patient	Ephesians 4:2
Gives freely	2 Corinthians 8:2; 1 John 3:17
Serves others	Galatians 5:13; 1 Thess 1:3; Hebrews 6:10
Promotes Unity	Philippians 2:2; Colossians 2:2; 3:14
Forgives	1 Peter 4:8
Is expressed in our actions	1 John 3:18
Overcomes fear	1 John 4:18

1 Corinthians 13 – The Love Chapter

When studying and meditating on the characteristics of biblical love, the singular chapter that captures it best is 1 Corinthians 13. Below is Apostle Paul's rendition of the God-kind of love from 1 Corinthians 13:4–8a NIV.

"Love is patient, love is kind. It does not envy, it does not boast, it is not proud. It does not dishonor others, it is not self-seeking, it is not easily angered, it keeps no record of wrongs. Love does not delight in evil but rejoices with the truth. It always protects, always trusts, always hopes, always perseveres. Love never fails."

Using the NIV translation, we see that there are eight things that love does and eight things that love does not do.

Love is	Love is NOT
Patient	Envious
Kind	Boastful
Joyful for what is true	Proud
Protective	Dishonoring of others
Trustworthy	Self-seeking
Hopeful	Easily angered
Persevering	A record keeper
Unfailing	Pleased with evil

"We are to do everything in love"

LOVE EVERYONE, EVERY TIME

We are to do everything in love (1 Corinthians 16:14). And everything really means everything—talking, working, eating, playing, training, correcting, etc.

And we should exhibit these characteristics, not only to those who are kind and loving toward us but even to our enemies. Jesus commands us to love the people who irritate us, get on our last nerve, disrespect us, and even try to harm us (Matthew 5:43–44). Now, this does not mean that we open the door and invite disaster and danger to dine with us, but it means that we extend grace, forgiveness, and patience where it was lacking. When necessary, we establish healthy boundaries while continuing to pray for our enemies and resist the urge to retaliate. We do not curse them or call down thunder to zap them out (Luke 6:35).

A few years ago, I read and re-read 1 Corinthians 13 almost every day for more than one month in response to a challenge given by a Pastor I listen to. I invite you to read, listen to, and meditate on this chapter consistently for as long as it takes for God's love to transform you and manifest in your actions in greater dimensions.

Consider using different versions of the Bible on different days for comparison, depth of study, and to gain a richer understanding of the text.

PRAYER

Father, help me take Your command to walk in love seriously and sincerely toward everyone. As I study and meditate on Your Word, fill me with a deeper understanding of what You require of me. Grant me the grace and daily strength to walk in obedience as I pursue loving others as Christ did, so that those around me may be drawn to You. In Jesus' name, Amen!.

1 Corinthians 13:1–8a

(From the AMPC translation)

1 If I [can] speak in the tongues of men and [even] of angels, but have not love (that reasoning, intentional, spiritual devotion such as is inspired by God's love for and in us), I am only a noisy gong or a clanging cymbal.

2 And if I have prophetic powers (the gift of interpreting the divine will and purpose), and understand all the secret truths and mysteries and possess all knowledge, and if I have [sufficient] faith so that I can remove mountains, but have not love (God's love in me) I am nothing (a useless nobody).

3 Even if I dole out all that I have [to the poor in providing] food, and if I surrender my body to be burned or in order that I may glory, but have not love (God's love in me), I gain nothing.

4 Love endures long and is patient and kind; love never is envious nor boils over with jealousy, is not boastful or vainglorious, does not display itself haughtily.

5 It is not conceited (arrogant and inflated with pride); it is not rude (unmannerly) and does not act unbecomingly. Love (God's love in us) does not insist on its own rights or its own way, for it is not self-seeking; it is not touchy or fretful or resentful; it takes no account of the evil done to it [it pays no attention to a suffered wrong].

6 It does not rejoice at injustice and unrighteousness, but rejoices when right and truth prevail.

7 Love bears up under anything and everything that comes, is ever ready to believe the best of every person, its hopes are fadeless under all circumstances, and it endures everything [without weakening].

8 Love never fails [never fades out or becomes obsolete or comes to an end].

REFLECT

† How does the Bible's definition of love challenge or reshape your understanding of what it means to truly love others?

† In what ways can you practice the kind of selfless, sacrificial love described in Scripture in your daily life?

† How did Jesus model biblical love, and what specific examples from His life inspire you to love more like Him?

† Are there relationships in your life where biblical love is needed right now? What steps can you take to show that love?

5

Love is a Fruit of the Holy Spirit

"But the fruit of the Spirit is love, joy, peace, forbearance, kindness, goodness, faithfulness, gentleness and self-control. Against such things there is no law." Galatians 5:22–23 NIV

In the last chapter, we defined biblical love using 1 Corinthians 13. And we can all agree that we cannot generate this type of sacrificial love by willpower or effort. God is love (1 John 4:8). Love comes from God and is imparted into our hearts by the Holy Spirit. When we are born-again, we become new spiritual beings because of what Jesus accomplished on the cross for us (2 Corinthians 5:17). God removes our stony hearts and gives us hearts that can respond to His love and love others (Jeremiah 31:33; Ezekiel 11:19).

"The Holy Spirit produces fruit in the lives of those who are born-again and yielded to Him."

The Holy Spirit moves in to dwell permanently in us (1 Corinthians 6:19).

He is the One who saturates our hearts with God's love and empowers us to love others.

> "And hope does not put us to shame, because God's love has been poured into our hearts through the Holy Spirit who has been given to us." Romans 5:5 ESV

> "For God gave us a spirit not of fear but of power and love and self-control." 2 Timothy 1:7 ESV

Without Him, we would revert to selfishness, making our love walk futile. Therefore, walking in love is a fruit or product of the Holy Spirit. It is not merely behavioral modification or striving to become our best selves.

> "Beloved, let us love one another, for love is from God, and whoever loves has been born of God and knows God." 1 John 4:7 ESV

"Just like a branch cannot bear fruit unless it remains connected to the vine, we cannot walk in love unless we abide in Christ and yield our lives to Him."

"Now that you have purified yourselves by obeying the truth so that you have sincere love for each other, love one another deeply, from the heart. For you have been born-again, not of perishable seed, but of imperishable, through the living and enduring word of God." 1 Peter 1:22–23 NIV

Did you notice that both Scriptures state that the only reason we can love is because we are born-again? God gave us the Holy Spirit and poured His love into our hearts to enable us to do the impossible—such as loving Him and others. If you identify as a born-again believer but do not manifest the love of God, ask God to show you what the problem is, then humble yourself and obey Him.

Cultivate the Fruit of Love by Abiding in Christ

God has given us the Holy Spirit, but we must remain connected to Him and allow Him to direct us. In John 15:5, Jesus said, "I am the vine; you are the branches. If you remain in me and I in you, you will bear much fruit; apart from me you can do nothing" (NIV). Some versions of the Bible, such as the NKJV, use the word 'abide' instead of 'remain.'

Abiding means maintaining an intimate, consistent, and unbroken relationship with Jesus Christ and the Holy Spirit. We do not visit with Jesus or put Him on time-out; instead, we yield to His leading. We spend time with Him in worship, prayer, and through the Word, so that we are prepared to respond in love when people or circumstances squeeze us.

PUTTING ON LOVE

Love isn't just based on emotions; it's an act of will. We choose to yield to the Holy Spirit and obey Him when He prompts us to do something for someone as an expression of love. God has given us His Spirit to dwell within us permanently. Ultimately, we must decide on each occasion whether to act in love or to choose selfishness.

Colossians 3:14 says, "And over all these virtues put on love, which binds them all together in perfect unity" (NIV). And 1 Thessalonians 5:8 says, "But since we belong to the day, let us be sober, putting on faith and love as a breastplate, and the hope of salvation as a helmet" (NIV).

We must decide to put on love—it's an act of our will.

"In very challenging situations, when we are interacting with people who are difficult to love, we need to seek God for wisdom and grace to love effectively."

There are different ways the Holy Spirit may prompt us to put on love, depending on the circumstances and the individuals we encounter. In very challenging situations, when we are interacting with people who are difficult to love, we need to seek God for wisdom and grace to love effectively.

PRACTICAL WAYS TO PUT ON LOVE

Putting on love may require you to pray for your offender and forgive (Matthew 5:44). Forgiving someone means they no longer owe you anything and that you choose to release them in both your thoughts and actions. Reconciliation is not always possible, but forgiveness is. You may need to speak with your offender and discuss the situation with them, and you might need to take a witness as instructed by the Bible (Matthew 18:15-16). Regardless of how the discussion unfolds, you need to speak the truth in love (Ephesians 4:15). The Bible also suggests that we may need to overlook an offense by figuratively turning the other cheek or going the extra mile (Matthew 5:38-41).

As I mentioned earlier, walking in love does not mean that you open the door for danger to dine and sleep with you.

A biblical illustration of this principle is found in the relationship between David and King Saul. When the first King of Israel, Saul, became extremely jealous of David because of his rising popularity, and wanted to kill him, David didn't linger—he ran for his life (1 Samuel 19:10-12). David protected himself and kept a safe distance.

On two occasions, David had the opportunity to kill Saul but chose not to retaliate (1 Samuel 24:3–15; 1 Samuel 26). David loved Saul and even called him "my father" after he spared his life in the cave.

> "See, my father, see the corner of your robe in my hand. For by the fact that I cut off the corner of your robe and did not kill you, you may know and see that there is no wrong or treason in my hands. I have not sinned against you, though you hunt my life to take it." 1 Samuel 24:11 ESV

When Saul and his son, Jonathan, died in battle, David mourned deeply, demonstrating his profound affection for a man who had wronged him (2 Samuel 1:11–12).

Just like David, there are some people for whom you will need to establish safe boundaries. However, even setting boundaries must be done on the foundation of love. If we are always building walls to keep people away from us and then claim we are setting boundaries, we may need to examine our motives for selfishness.

In the same conversation where Jesus instructs us to take witnesses when confronting an offender, He continued the discussion by stating that, "If they still refuse to listen, tell it to the church; and if they refuse to listen even to the church, treat them as you would a pagan or a tax collector" (Matthew 18:17). As you can see, Jesus wants us to do our part and everything necessary to live peacefully and lovingly with others. We are to do everything in love (1 Corinthians 16:14) and within our power to maintain peace.

We cannot force our opponents to love us, but as far as it depends on us, God calls us to live in peace with others (Romans 12:18).

THINK ON THIS

Love is a fruit of the Holy Spirit. None of us will successfully bear the fruit of love unless we are born-again and yield to the work of the Holy Spirit. We cultivate God's love within us by abiding in Christ and choosing to embrace love when the Holy Spirit prompts us.

No, it's not an easy road. But we can do it because the same power that raised Jesus Christ from the dead lives in us (Romans 8:11). And if we fail, God has promised in 1 John 1:9 that "if we confess our sins, he is faithful and just and will forgive us our sins and purify us from all unrighteousness" (NIV).

PRAYER

In the words of Apostle Paul from Philippians 1:9-10 NIV, "this is my prayer: that your love may abound more and more in knowledge and depth of insight, so that you may be able to discern what is best and may be pure and blameless for the day of Christ." In Jesus' name, Amen!

REFLECT

✝ How is the love produced by the Holy Spirit different from the love we try to show on our own strength?

✝ In what ways have you seen the Holy Spirit grow the fruit of love in your life over time?

✝ Are there areas in your heart where you are resisting the Spirit's work of love? What might it look like to surrender those areas to God?

✝ How can you stay connected to the Spirit daily so that love becomes a natural overflow of your relationship with Christ?

6

Love: A Key to Spiritual Growth

"Dear friends, let us love one another, for love comes from God. Everyone who loves has been born of God and knows God. Whoever does not love does not know God, because God is love." 1 John 4:7-8 (NIV)

The Apostle John tells us three important truths in the verse above:

1. Everyone who loves is born of God.

2. We should love one another because love is of God.

3. He who does not love does not KNOW God.

A great way to measure our spiritual growth and test whether we are in the faith is by closely examining our love walk (2 Corinthians 13:5).

The Greek word for love used in these verses is agape, which is the highest form of love. It means selfless, unconditional, God-kind of love. Believers in Jesus are commanded to love others, not based on how we feel at the moment or whether they deserve it or not. Rather, we love because:

† God has loved us unconditionally (Ephesians 5:1-2),

† We love God (1 John 4:11), and

† Our desire as God's children is to please Him (John 14:21).

WE ARE COMMANDED TO LOVE

In John 15:12, Jesus commands us to love one another as He has loved us. In John 13:34–35, He takes it further by telling us an important truth: His disciples will be identified by the visible demonstration of their love for one another!

"Our ability to love others reveals that we are not only born-again but also know God and are growing in our knowledge of Him."

"If anyone says, "I love God," and hates his brother, he is a liar; for he who does not love his brother whom he has seen cannot love God whom he has not seen." 1 John 4:20 ESV

Meditate and ponder on 1 John 4:20, then reflect on these questions.

Can we truly say we love God, yet we…

† can't stand our fellow sister or brother in Christ?

† are quick to gossip, backbite, harbor envy, and keep unforgiving feelings in our hearts toward one another?

† viciously attack others with our words and thoughts, targeting those who have hurt us, instead of responding as Matthew 5:44 suggests?

† refuse to respond in obedience to His instructions on how to live our lives by His word?

In Matthew 22:38–40, Jesus gave us two commandments:

† Love God with all of your being, and

† Love your neighbor as yourself.

We understand that loving God means obeying Him. Loving people involves treating everyone in a way that reflects the presence of the fruit of the Spirit in our lives (Galatians 5: 22-23, 1 Corinthians 13:4-8).

"Loving God means obeying Him."

Treating people this way is an act of obedience to God

(1 Corinthians 16:14, Hebrews 13:1).

As our love for God grows and our knowledge of Him deepens, so should our obedience to Him increase (Philippians 1:9-11). The way we treat others should reflect our ever-increasing love for God. Our hearts ought to become more tender and responsive to the leading of His Holy Spirit within us—never making excuses to remain in willful disobedience to the One whom we say we love.

One way to determine if we are growing spiritually is to examine ourselves in this area. We should be able to look back and see if we are growing in our obedience to Him, and therefore growing in our love for Him and for all people.

PRAYER

Father, You love me immeasurably and unconditionally. Please forgive me for the times I have treated others unfairly and unkindly, whether deliberately or unknowingly. I desire to grow spiritually and be used as Your vessel to reach the lost and encourage the weary. Strengthen, guide, and equip me to be quick to obey when You prompt me to choose love in my daily interactions. In Jesus' name, Amen!

REFLECT

✝ How have you seen love—or a lack of it—affect your spiritual growth?

✝ In what specific ways can you grow in loving others more like Christ this week?

✝ Are there attitudes or habits in your life that hinder you from loving others as God calls you to?

✝ How can you allow God's love to transform not just your actions, but your heart and mindset?

7

Unlocking Forgiveness Through God's Love

I was deeply hurt by someone a while ago. You know the kind of hurt that penetrates your bone marrow and leaves you feeling as if your heart weighs a thousand pounds.

Afterward, I followed the 'right' steps. I prayed and handed it to God. However, the hurt didn't go away. Instead, it lingered, allowing unforgiveness to creep into my heart. I tried hard to shake it off and move on, but I was tormented by negative thoughts. My spirit wanted to forgive, but my flesh desired lightning to flash from heaven and strike this person.

Finally, God captured my attention with His unconditional love for me through a song on my playlist. A segment of the lyrics of the song 'Perfect Love' by Jesus Culture goes like this:

"Perfect love, perfect love, it's perfect love.
Breaks down walls, casts out fear.
It's perfect love. Unconditional, freely given.
Yeah, perfect love.
His name is Jesus, His name is Jesus!"

—*Jesus Culture, "Perfect Love"*

I was reminded that God's love for me is perfect. God loves me deeply, unconditionally, and personally. No amount of mistreatment or hurt by anyone can diminish His love for me (Romans 8:38–39).

As I meditated on His love for me, my heart healed, and my hurts melted away. With a healed heart, I was able to approach my offender with the overflow of God's love within me and see him/her through the lens of God's love. Then, I rejoiced in the truth and reality that God's love does cover a multitude of sins (1 Peter 4:8).

WHAT DOES THE BIBLE TEACH ON FORGIVENESS AND LOVE?

No one is born holy and righteous. We all come into this world as sinners (Romans 3:23). The Scriptures make it clear that "there is no one righteous, not even one" (Romans 3:10 NIV).

Compared to the glory of God, our human attempts at holiness are like filthy rags (Isaiah 64:6). God is holy and perfect (1 Samuel 2:2). Therefore, our sinful nature separated us from Him and prevented us from relating to Him (Isaiah 59:2).

But because of His great love for us, God sent His Son into this world to redeem us from our sins and reconcile us to an intimate love relationship with Himself through Jesus' sacrifice on the cross (John 3:16, Ephesians 2:4–5). He didn't wait for us to clean up our act. Instead, He offered Jesus while we were still sinners (Romans 5:8). Jesus is the picture of perfect love because He gave Himself as a sacrifice to God for us (Ephesians 5:2).

In addition, because of His love for us, God has granted us total and complete forgiveness of our sins in Christ Jesus (Ephesians 1:7, Colossians 1:14). This forgiveness is entirely based on His grace, not on our ability to earn it (Ephesians 2:8). It is freely available to all who repent of their sins and receive it by faith (Acts 2:38, 20:21).

His forgiveness does not end at the point of salvation. If we sin afterward, Jesus serves as our advocate before God, and

His sacrifice still speaks for us (1 John 2:1-2). If we confess our sins, God is faithful to forgive us and purify us from all unrighteousness (1 John 1:9).

As if the riches of His love and grace toward us weren't enough, He made us new, took away our old sin nature, and put His Spirit within us (2 Corinthians 5:17). We are the temples of the Living God, and the Holy Spirit dwells in us (1 Corinthians 3:16, 6:19). Because we have His Spirit within us, we possess His power to extend the same love and forgiveness He offered to us to others (Galatians 5:22).

God is love, and He has poured His love into our hearts through His Spirit (Romans 5:5). As we spend time in His presence and meditate on Scriptures concerning His love for us, we are empowered through His Spirit who dwells within us to walk in His love and forgive others just as He forgave us.

"Because of His love for us, God has granted us total and complete forgiveness of our sins in Christ Jesus."

Ten Bible Verses on Forgiveness and Love

A. God's Love and Forgiveness

i.   "In this is love, not that we have loved God but that he loved us and sent his Son to be the propitiation for our sins." 1 John 4:10 ESV

ii.   "...but God shows his love for us in that while we were still sinners, Christ died for us." Romans 5:8 ESV

iii.   "But God, being rich in mercy, because of the great love with which he loved us, even when we were dead in our trespasses, made us alive together with Christ—by grace you have been saved." Ephesians 2:4–5 ESV

iv.   "But when the goodness and loving kindness of God our Savior appeared, he saved us, not because of works done by us in righteousness, but according to his own mercy, by the washing of regeneration and renewal of the Holy Spirit." Titus 3:4-5 ESV

v. "He does not deal with us according to our sins, nor repay us according to our iniquities. For as high as the heavens are above the earth, so great is his steadfast love toward those who fear him." Psalms 103:10-11 ESV

vi. "I, I am he who blots out your transgressions for my own sake, and I will not remember your sins." Isaiah 43:25 ESV

B. OUR RESPONSE TO GOD'S LOVE AND FORGIVENESS

vii. "Love prospers when a fault is forgiven, but dwelling on it separates close friends." Proverbs 17:9 NLT

viii. "Be kind to one another, tenderhearted, forgiving one another, as God in Christ forgave you." Ephesians 4:32 ESV

ix. "Therefore be imitators of God, as beloved children. And walk in love, as Christ loved us and gave himself up for us, a fragrant offering and sacrifice to God." Ephesians 5:1–2 ESV

x. "Put on then, as God's chosen ones, holy and beloved, compassionate hearts, kindness, humility, meekness, and patience, bearing with one another and, if one has a complaint against another, forgiving each other; as the Lord has forgiven you, so you also must forgive. And above all these put on love, which binds everything together in perfect harmony." Colossians 3:12-14 ESV

PRACTICAL STEPS TO FORGIVENESS

Repent, confess your sin, and ask God for forgiveness (1 John 1:9).

Pray for your adversaries (Mark 11:25).

Bless and do not curse (Romans 12:14).

Speak the word over the situation. Whenever you are reminded of the hurts caused by another, confess your love for them by faith and speak God's word over them.

"Love is the key that unlocks forgiveness."

Meditate on God's Word, nurturing your spirit with His love and forgiveness. The stronger your spirit is in accepting God's love and forgiveness for you, the easier it will be to forgive others. Live each day with the awareness that Jesus Christ Himself lives in you (Colossians 1:27).

Love is the key that unlocks forgiveness, and God has poured His love into your heart (Romans 5:5). The choice is now yours to tap into His love and refresh others with it.

You are more than a conqueror (Romans 8:37), and you can walk in forgiveness.

Receive God's Word (James 1:21). Believe you can do it, then obey and exercise your faith by offering forgiveness in love to others.

THINK ON THIS

I thank God for His love for me. He loves me even in my imperfections as He leads me to His perfection. I thank Him for forgiving my sins, making me His child, giving me His Spirit, and granting me the grace to extend the same forgiveness to others.

The same is true for you. As you have received God's love and forgiveness, depend on Him for the grace to extend the same to others. It's a process, but you're not alone–He's with you every step of the way.

LORD, You are a good God, and we love You!

PRAYER

Father, I thank You for loving me perfectly, even in my imperfections. Thank You for the forgiveness You freely offer and for the grace that empowers me to extend that same forgiveness to others. I confess that I can't do this on my own–I need You. Strengthen me through Your Holy Spirit to love those who have hurt me, to bless and not curse, and to release every offense into Your hands. Let Your Word shape my thoughts, my actions, and my responses. I choose today to walk in love and to forgive, just as You have forgiven me. In Jesus' name, Amen.

REFLECT

† What does God's love teach you about the true nature of forgiveness?

† How has receiving God's forgiveness impacted your ability to forgive yourself and others?

† Are there any unresolved areas in your heart where forgiveness is needed? How might God's love help you take a step toward healing?

† In what ways can walking in God's love empower you to forgive even when it feels undeserved or painful?

8

Love Is The Greatest

"And now these three remain: faith, hope and love. But the greatest of these is love." 1 Corinthians 13:13 NIV

When facing important decisions, we often turn to a familiar tool: a list of the pros and cons. On the pro side, we list reasons to act, while on the con side, we consider reasons to pause or walk away.

However, when the question is to love or not, such a list becomes unnecessary because doing everything in love guarantees God's blessings. Embracing love means aligning with God Himself. Love is the greatest of all divine virtues because God is love.

Love is the driving force behind all other spiritual virtues.

Love is the greatest of all divine virtues because God is love.

In Hebrews 11:6, we're told that "without faith, it is impossible to please God" (NIV). That's a powerful truth! However, as essential and powerful as faith is, it cannot function effectively without love because faith and love are intricately connected.

> "For in Christ Jesus neither circumcision nor uncircumcision counts for anything, but only faith working through love."
> Galatians 5:6 ESV

Placing our trust in God requires that we believe in His goodness and rest in His love. If we are not drawing strength from His love, our faith will eventually falter.

Even if our faith can move mountains, if it is not accompanied by love, as Paul stated in 1 Corinthians 13:2, we become nothing more than whitewashed tombs that display the outward signs of Christianity but whose hearts are not genuinely yielded to God. The result is lives that bear no lasting fruit in the Kingdom of God.

This connection between faith and love extends into everyday life. If you're praying for God to restore a relationship or bless your finances, you must practice Christlike love—especially in how you treat others.

After all, what good is it to pray for more customers for your business if you're rude or dismissive to the ones you already have? As a dentist who treats patients with chronic facial pain and oral lesions, I rely on the Holy Spirit to guide me in treating my patients with care and love. And when I falter, I ask for forgiveness and keep moving forward.

Similarly, love is the force that unites all the other fruits of the Spirit (Galatians 5:22-23). If we choose to neglect letting love guide our decisions and actions, we will ultimately lose our joy, peace, and all the other fruits of the Spirit.

In addition, perfect love drives fear from our hearts. Fear and timidity do not come from God (2 Timothy 1:7). Those who belong to Jesus, follow Him, and understand how deeply God loves them are no longer tormented by the fear of God's judgment or condemnation (Romans 8:1). We fear God in the sense that we love Him, respect Him, obey Him, and are in awe of His splendor and majesty. However, we are not afraid that He will snuff us out and send us to eternal damnation because we have already wholeheartedly accepted Jesus' sacrifice on the cross as payment for our sins. Even in challenging situations, we learn to trust and rely on God's love and His promises that He will never leave us nor forsake us.

"When our hearts are secure in God's love, we become willing vessels, able to love freely, live courageously, and extend grace to others."

He will help, strengthen, fight for, shield, deliver, console, and comfort us.

We also do not hold back from loving others with the same love we have received from God because we know that God is our Provider and Protector. His perfect love drives out fear—including the fear of rejection, failure, and inadequacy. When we truly understand how deeply and unconditionally God loves us, we no longer live controlled by the opinions or approval of others. Instead, we are anchored in the truth that our identity and worth come from Him alone. This frees us to interact with others in a gracious and kind way, not from a need to be accepted, but from a place of already being fully accepted by God.

Knowing God's love also transforms how we perceive ourselves. We no longer feel the need to hide our weaknesses or imperfections because we understand that we are fully known and still fully loved by our Creator. This acceptance gives us the courage to step out in faith, try new things, and take bold actions without being paralyzed by fear of failure. When our hearts are secure in God's love, we become willing vessels, able to love freely, live courageously, and extend grace to others—even when it's difficult—because we know we are drawing from an infinite source of love that never runs out.

"By this is love perfected with us, so that we may have confidence for the day of judgment, because as he is so also are we in this world. There is no fear in love, but perfect love casts out fear. For fear has to do with punishment, and whoever fears has not been perfected in love." 1 John 4:17-

"Love never fails," so let us choose daily to "follow the way of love" (1 Corinthians 13:8;14:1 NIV).

CONCLUSION

If this were a debate in my elementary school, I would conclude with this line: "With these few points of mine, I hope I have been able to convince you to choose love daily."

But seriously, I hope this book has awakened in you a deeper hunger to know God more intimately—to be transformed by His love in a way that changes how you think, speak, and live, leaving a lasting impact on your life and those around you.

PRAYER

Father, thank You for choosing to love me. Forgive me for the times I have not fully embraced Your mercy and grace. I do not want to be a fake Christian who puts on a facade of holiness while my heart remains unchanged by Your love. I choose to walk in Your divine love rather than in my own interpretation of what love looks like. Purify my heart of jealousy, pride, unforgiveness, and other selfish traits. Grant me a deeper revelation of Your love and the wisdom I need for every encounter. Empower me through Your Spirit to be a vessel through which those in my world experience Your love. In Jesus' name, Amen!

REFLECT

✝ What does it mean in your life that "love is the greatest?" How can you make love your primary focus in your decisions and relationships?

✝ How can allowing love to guide your thoughts and actions help you grow in the other fruits of the Spirit, like joy, peace, and kindness?

✝ How does your faith express itself in love for others, particularly those who are difficult to love?

✝ Is fear preventing you from moving forward in any part of your life? How can God's love set you free to fulfill everything He has called you to do?

† How does the promise that "love never fails" encourage you to continue loving even when it's challenging or doesn't seem to yield immediate results?

SALVATION PRAYER

If you are not yet a follower of Jesus, I implore you to have a change of heart. Repent and commit your life to Him TODAY.

The benefits of walking with Jesus are eternal, and so are the consequences of rejecting Him.

You can pray in your own words or use the prayer below as a guide.

Father,

I ask You to forgive me of my sins. Specifically, I repent for rejecting Jesus as my Savior.

Today, I confess with my mouth that Jesus is Lord, and I wholeheartedly believe in my heart that You raised Him from the dead to give me eternal life.

I lay my life down, and I receive Jesus Christ as my Lord and Savior.

I commit to follow Jesus and obey Him all the days of my life. In Jesus' name, I pray.

Amen.

About The Author

Dr. Chizobam Idahosa is a wife, a mother to three beautiful girls, and a dentist who is triple-board-certified in oral medicine, orofacial pain, and lifestyle medicine. At the core of her identity, she sees herself as a child of the Most-High God and a servant of Christ Jesus.

Chizobam is passionate about studying, meditating, and teaching the Word. In 2015, she founded Beautiful in Jesus, a Christian ministry that emerged from her journey toward inward beauty and spiritual maturity through the study of God's Word. Beautiful in Jesus equips believers with practical, biblical truths to help them know God more intimately and walk in step with the Holy Spirit as He transforms them into the image of Christ. Chizobam invites you to connect with her at www.BeautifulinJesus.com and sign up to receive her weekly email devotionals.

Social Links

⌁ beautifulinjesus.com

⌁ facebook.com/beautifulinjesus

⌁ instagram.com/beautifulinjesus/

⌁ pinterest.com/beautifulinjesus

⌁ youtube.com/@beautifulinjesus